YOUR KNOWLEDGE HAS VALUE

- We will publish your bachelor's and master's thesis, essays and papers

- Your own eBook and book - sold worldwide in all relevant shops

- Earn money with each sale

Upload your text at www.GRIN.com and publish for free

Bibliographic information published by the German National Library:

The German National Library lists this publication in the National Bibliography; detailed bibliographic data are available on the Internet at http://dnb.dnb.de .

This book is copyright material and must not be copied, reproduced, transferred, distributed, leased, licensed or publicly performed or used in any way except as specifically permitted in writing by the publishers, as allowed under the terms and conditions under which it was purchased or as strictly permitted by applicable copyright law. Any unauthorized distribution or use of this text may be a direct infringement of the author s and publisher s rights and those responsible may be liable in law accordingly.

Imprint:

Copyright © 2015 GRIN Verlag
Print and binding: Books on Demand GmbH, Norderstedt Germany
ISBN: 9783668662988

This book at GRIN:

https://www.grin.com/document/416290

Anne Sander

The themes of several classic novels and plays

About Bram Stoker's "Dracula", William Shakespeare's "A Midsummer Night's Dream", Oscar Wilde's "The Importance of Being Earnest" etc.

GRIN Verlag

GRIN - Your knowledge has value

Since its foundation in 1998, GRIN has specialized in publishing academic texts by students, college teachers and other academics as e-book and printed book. The website www.grin.com is an ideal platform for presenting term papers, final papers, scientific essays, dissertations and specialist books.

Visit us on the internet:

http://www.grin.com/

http://www.facebook.com/grincom

http://www.twitter.com/grin_com

Johann-Wolfgang-Goethe-Universität Frankfurt am Main
Institute for English and American Studies
Literaturwissenschaften
WS2015/2016

The Themes of Classics

This paper will analyze the different themes of several classic novels and plays. The examined works are Bram Stoker's *Dracula*, William Shakespeare's *A Midsummer Night's Dream*, Oscar Wilde's *The Importance of Being Earnest*, Arthur Conan Doyle's *The Hound of the Baskervilles*, and the two short stories from James Joyce's *Dubliners*, "Evelin" and "Counterparts".

The Themes of *Dracula*

The novel *Dracula* was written in 1897 by Bram Stoker. The themes of religion, superstition, imprisonment and love are addressed.

The first theme is religion. Count Dracula, as a vampire, represents all the evil in a Christian world. He does not only drink blood but can communicate with wolves, is very strong, has no shadow or reflection in a mirror, can transform himself into a wolf, a bat, mist or the moonlight. The best way to protect oneself in *Dracula* is with either a crucifix, a communion wafer, or other Christian items but also ordinary objects like garlic or a wooden stake can help. Both, the figurative drinking of blood and resurrection are important themes in Christianity. Dracula, however, deforms these themes by drinking actual blood and being undead.

The second theme is superstition. While London is very advanced and progressive, the villages in the Carpathian Mountains are not. The people are still very superstitious, in fact "[…] every known superstition in the world is gathered […]" (Stoker 8) there. When Harker arrives in Bistritz, the people cross themselves when he asks for Count Dracula and the old lady of the inn gives him a crucifix to protect him against evil. It shows the contrast between the scientific and modern London and the primitive and superstitious Transylvania. Van Helsing can be seen as a bridge between those two places since he is a man of science, who fits into the world of London, but also a man with great knowledge of superstitions and the supernatural.

The next theme is imprisonment. After a few days Jonathan Harker realizes that he cannot leave the Count's castle. All the doors are locked so his only escape route are the windows. However, the castle is built on a cliff which makes this exit very dangerous. Once Jonathan realizes that he is a prisoner of the Count, he feels helpless. This helplessness enables him to take the risk of falling to his death and he escapes through a window. Another prisoner is Lucy Westenra. Even though she is not held captive in the Count's castle she is imprisoned in her own body, once Dracula starts drinking her blood. She has no control over her own movements and is often caught sleepwalking by Mina. Even after she dies, she is still imprisoned because she is a vampire. She is only liberated when Arthur kills her. Mina Harker is imprisoned by Dracula, like Lucy is, if not as severe. She still has control over her body, but not over her mind. Mina and Dracula are connected, so Van Helsing often hypnotizes her to find out information about the Count. She is freed when Dracula dies.

Another theme is love. There are two couples in Dracula, Jonathan and Mina and Arthur and Lucy. However, Arthur is not the only one who loves Lucy. She gets three different proposals from Arthur, Dr. Seward and Quincey Morris in one day. She chooses Arthur, even though she wants to marry all of them. Lucy is also loved by Mina, who is her best friend. If it were not for all the people who love her, Lucy would have turned into a vampire a lot earlier. Of course, she still dies in the end, even though her friends did everything they could. Mina, however, is saved by her friends. Like Lucy, she is loved by her husband and her friends. Quincey's last thoughts are about Mina before he dies and even Van Helsing loves her and wants to protect her. Love can be helpful in *Dracula* but it does not guarantee one's survival.

The Themes of *A Midsummer Night's Dream*

A Midsummer Night's Dream (presumably 1595/1596) is a comedy written by William Shakespeare. The original date of its completion is unknown, but it is assumable that the earliest possible publication could be in 1594 and the latest in 1598 (Holland 110). The play consists of five acts, in which love, marriage, magic and performance are important themes.

A very prominent theme of the play is love. The main love interest shifts throughout the story. At first Hermia is the object of desire, but after Lysander and Demetrius are enchanted it is now Helena. In the end, a new balance is created when Lysander is in love with Hermia again. Hermia and Lysander are in love, while Demetrius is also in love with Hermia and Hermia's friend Helena is in love with Demetrius. After Puck enchants Lysander and Demetrius, however, they are now both in love with Helena. This leads to a lot of jealousy, because suddenly both men who were previously in love with Hermia do not care for her at all, but are

Johann-Wolfgang-Goethe-Universität Frankfurt am Main
Institute for English and American Studies
Literaturwissenschaften
WS2015/2016

trying to win over Helena. The men are so in love that they want to fight over Helena and Lysander actually offers Helena to kill Hermia. In the end Lysander gets cured of the love spell and can be with Hermia, while Demetrius continues to love Helena, who is still in love with him.

Another theme, similar to love, is marriage. At the beginning Hermia is forced, by her father Egeus, to marry Demetrius, which she refuses and runs away with Lysander instead. Demetrius was engaged to Hermia's friend Helena and is now engaged to Hermia. Not including Pyramus and Thisbe, there are four couples in the story, of which one is already married and the remaining three get married in the end. Oberon and Titania are king and queen of the fairies, while Hermia and Lysander, and Helena and Demetrius marry at the same time as Theseus and Hippolyta. Even though Oberon and Titania are married, they do not love each other and are fighting over an Indian boy. With the help of the love potion, the king made her fall in love with the transformed Bottom, for his own amusement and as a distraction so Oberon can take the boy from her.

Magic is another one of the play's themes. One magical creature of the play is Puck. He is the servant of Oberon, the Fairy King and has different magic abilities. He transforms Bottom, he is invisible, he imitates the voices of Lysander and Demetrius and Puck changes the weather so that the two men cannot find each other in the dark. The love potion is an essential part of the story. It comes from a flower that got shot by Cupid's arrow. The juice from this flower can make anyone fall in love with the first person they see after they awake. It is a key element to the play and triggers the entire conflict between the four young lovers. The love potion affects Lysander, Demetrius and Titania, but only she and Lysander get cured with an antidote. Demetrius stays enchanted and in love with Helena.

At last, there is the theme of performance. Almost the entire fifth act consists of a play within a play. The mechanicals are performing the drama of Pyramus and Thisbe, a story which resembles the story of the four protagonists. However, the mechanicals are not talented actors and perform rather poorly.

Johann-Wolfgang-Goethe-Universität Frankfurt am Main
Institute for English and American Studies
Literaturwissenschaften
WS2015/2016

The Themes of *The Importance of Being Earnest*

The Importance of Being Earnest (1895) is a play written by Oscar Wilde. It consists of three acts and deals with the themes of irony, superficiality and lies.

Irony is an important theme of the play. Jack assures Gwendolen that his name certainly is John but Gwendolen only wants to marry someone named Ernest. It is ironic that Jack's actual name is Ernest John, allowing him to marry Gwendolen. It is also ironic that Ernest says "I never had a brother in my life, and I certainly have not the smallest intention of ever having one in the future" (Wilde 56) but right after he discovers that Algernon is in fact his younger brother he says "I knew I had a brother! I always said I had a brother" (Wilde 72-73).

The superficiality of the characters is very prominent. Gwendolen and Cecily are focused on the names of their fiancés; they both want to marry someone called Ernest. Lady Bracknell allows Algernon to marry Cecily only after she hears how much money Cecily has. When Lady Bracknell interviews Ernest to see if he should marry Gwendolen, she does not enquire about his personality or love for Gwendolen but rather his income and estates. The only reason she has to reject Ernest, is that he is an orphan and was found in a handbag at Victoria Station.

The characters lie a lot, especially Algernon and Ernest. They lie to get away from their boring lives. Ernest uses the name Jack when he is with Cecily and the name Ernest when he is with Algernon. Algernon uses Bunbury, a sickly man he invented to escape to the country as often as he can. Miss Prism lied about confusing the baby and her book. She is the reason for this confusion.

The Themes of "The Hound of the Baskervilles"

The Hound of the Baskervilles was written in 1902 by Arthur Conan Doyle. It is a novel focusing on the themes of lying, the natural and unnatural, and the moor.

The first important theme is lying. Many characters lie about something. Holmes told Watson that he is in London while he actually was in Dartmoor. Mr. Stapleton lies about his sister who is not actually his sister but his wife. He also hides the fact that he is an heir of Hugo Baskerville and the one behind the murders. The butler Barrymore and his wife keep her brother, the escaped convict Selden, hidden.

The line between the natural and the unnatural is another theme. The Baskervilles are not cursed. It is Stapleton who wants to kill Sir Henry and every other rival to his inheritance. The hound is no supernatural beast that haunts the Baskervilles. It is an ordinary dog painted with phosphorus so it would glow in the dark and scare people to death. Holmes is convinced that the murders have a scientific explanation but even a "trained man of science" (Doyle 17) like Dr. Mortimer considers the murders to be supernatural.

The next theme is the moor itself. It is a dark, remote and eerie place with few inhabitants. It is also the perfect location for a murder. This atmosphere makes the supernatural aspect of the murders much more plausible. The moor is a dangerous place, not only because of Selden and the hound, but because it is Stapleton's cause of death when he left the safe path and drowned in the moor.

The Themes of "Eveline"

Eveline is the fourth short story in James Joyce's *Dubliners*. It was published in 1914 and focuses on nostalgia and the fear of leaving.

The first theme is nostalgia. Eveline thinks about all the things that once were, when she was still happy. The field that she and her brothers used to play in is gone. Her mother was still alive and her father was nicer. Most of her friends have either moved away or dead. Eveline has decided to leave her home, like all her other friends did, and go to Buenos Aires with Frank. Until the end she is unsure whether to actually leave or stay, which results in her abandoning Frank in the station.

The second theme is the fear of leaving. Eveline hopes that when she leaves for Buenos Aires she will be treated with more respect and have a better life. Her father is treating her very poorly and she struggles with financial problems. She has to work hard every day, so it would make sense for her to leave. Even though she could have lived a happy life with Frank in Argentina, Eveline decides against it. Before her mother died she promised her to keep the family together. With her one brother dead and her other brother gone, she and her father are the only ones left. If Eveline went to Buenos Aires she would leave her father behind, who would miss her. She would abandon the rest of her family and friends and the only life she has ever known. This is a scary thought and the reason why she decided against it.

Johann-Wolfgang-Goethe-Universität Frankfurt am Main
Institute for English and American Studies
Literaturwissenschaften
WS2015/2016

The Themes of "Counterparts"

The short story *Counterparts* is the ninth chapter of *Dubliners*, written by James Joyce in 1914. The two themes alcoholism and aggression are addressed.

Alcoholism is the first theme in this short story. Farrington is constantly thinking about having a drink. It interferes with his work and is causing trouble with his boss, which leads to him needing alcohol even more. His friends encourage this behaviour and take him to several bars. At work he can only think of going to pubs and drinking his worries away. Farrington's alcoholism does not only hold him back at his job but also ruins his marriage. At the bar he tries to flirt with a woman who then rejects him. His wife is also directly affected by his drunkenness since she is harassed by him when he is drunk. In return she harasses him when he is sober.

The second theme is aggression. Farrington's aggression is connected to his alcoholism. As soon as he starts drinking he gets more aggressive. But even when he is at the office he expresses rage against his boss. He knows that it is impossible for him to finish his task on time so he gets furious. He wants to destroy the office and hit his boss. His only consolation is the knowledge that he will be drinking with his friends this night. Even though he finally gets the drinks that he needs, he is still discontented. He is angry that he has to spend so much money and that he lost the arm wrestling competition with Weathers. When he comes home from the pub after he spend the night drinking and finds that there is no dinner prepared for him, he starts beating his son.

Johann-Wolfgang-Goethe-Universität Frankfurt am Main
Institute for English and American Studies
Literaturwissenschaften
WS2015/2016

Bibliography

Doyle, Arthur Conan. *The Hound of the Baskervilles*. n.p.: CreateSpace Independent Publishing Platform. 2013. Print.

Holland, Peter, ed. William Shakespeare. A Midsummer Night's Dream. New York: Oxford University Press. 1994. Print.

Joyce, James. *Dubliners*. London: Penguin Classics. 2000. Print.

Shakespeare, William. A Midsummer Night's Dream. Stuttgart: Reclam. 2013. Print.

Stoker, Bram. *Dracula*. London: Penguin Classics. 2003. Print.

Wilde, Oscar. *The Importance of Being Earnest*. n.p.: CreateSpace Independent Publishing Platform. 2016. Print.

YOUR KNOWLEDGE HAS VALUE

- We will publish your bachelor's and
  master's thesis, essays and papers

- Your own eBook and book -
  sold worldwide in all relevant shops

- Earn money with each sale

Upload your text at www.GRIN.com
and publish for free